# Open Hearts, Waiting Homes

An Adoption Devotional
for Families Preparing to Adopt

MICHELLE CROSS-FRASE

Owl's Head Publishers

Text copyright © 2016 by Michelle Cross-Frase

All rights reserved. No part of this book may be reproduced or transmitted in any form or by any means, electronic or mechanical, including photocopying, recording, or by any information storage and retrieval system, without the written permission of the Publisher, except where permitted by law.

All Scripture quotations, unless otherwise indicated, are taken from THE HOLY BIBLE, NEW INTERNATIONAL VERSION®, NIV® Copyright © 1973, 1978, 1984, 2011 by Biblica, Inc.™ Used by permission. All rights reserved worldwide.

Scripture quotations marked (NLT) are taken from the Holy Bible, New Living Translation, copyright © 1996, 2004, 2007 by Tyndale House Foundation. Used by permission of Tyndale House Publishers, Inc., Carol Stream, IL 60188. All rights reserved.

Copyright © 2016 Michelle Cross-Frase

All rights reserved.

ISBN: 0692618554
ISBN-13: 978-0692618554

# DEDICATION

For my daughters, whom I love deeply. For the man and woman who gave them life and provided a loving family for them until they tragically passed. For those in America and Uganda who played the greatest and seemingly insignificant roles in bringing these precious children into our hearts and home, because it could not have happened without each of you. For my husband, who has been the most beautiful father and supportive partner in this journey. For our family, who supported us through all the crazy moments in this process. And for the parents who have adoption on their hearts, for whom it is my prayer that you will soon see your dreams lived out as you wrap your arms around your child.

# ADOPTION
It was never Plan B.

# CONTENTS

Introduction ...................................................... 9
Your Family's Adoption Timeline ...................... 13
    Spirit of Adoption ........................................ 15
    Greater Than You Can Count...................... 19
    Entrusted to Your Care ................................ 22
    Sustaining the Fatherless ............................. 25
    Up Against an Army .................................... 28
    Patient or Pleading ...................................... 31
    A Love Question ......................................... 34
    Construction Process .................................. 37
    Will You Love Me? ..................................... 40
    Fighting Two Battles ................................... 43
    Compassion in Distress ............................... 46
    You've Been Sent ........................................ 50
    Growing the Heart and Head ..................... 53
    Time to Celebrate ....................................... 56
    Hard Choices .............................................. 59
    Bringing Down the Walls ........................... 63

Birth Family Fears ..........................................66
Heartbreak and Hope .....................................69
Inheritance ........................................................72
In Pursuit ..........................................................76
The Making of a Miracle ................................79
Exposed ............................................................82
An Unlikely Hero ............................................85
The Most Exciting Story ................................89
A Plan for Heavenly Adoption ......................94
About the Author ............................................96

Introduction

Since we are meeting through this book, I am guessing it is relatively safe to assume that your family or someone very dear to you is in the process of adopting a child or perhaps several children. Maybe you are in the initial phase of considering whether adoption is the right choice for your family.

Dear friend, let me tell you how much that excites my heart to know that your sacrificial love is hard at work creating a loving, permanent home for a child desperately seeking a family. I would love to have the opportunity to sit down with you, hear about your adoption journey, and share some time encouraging you in this process of growing a family.

Chances are we won't have such an opportunity on this side of Heaven. So I'd like to invite you to share some time through the pages of this book. I won't attempt to tell you I have all the answers, nor could I truly understand the struggles and joys you are experiencing in your family's unique adoption process.

To make the most of this devotional, I encourage you to have a Bible and a pen or pencil handy during your study time. Each devotion includes a short suggested reading from Scripture, along with a passage that I like to use as a snapshot of the story presented. You'll also find that there is a place at the beginning of each devotion to record the date. Months or years down the road, I can assure you that it will be such a blessing to be able to reminisce along the path you took to reach the realization of your adoption.

I encourage you to write all over the pages of this book. By design, I've provided some space for notes, records, thoughtful reflection, solid responses, and prayer topics. The suggestions for journaling are a reflection of the points I personally wish I had examined more closely as well as those areas which proved to be the most helpful to me during our family's adoption. There are questions you can ask yourself, providing prompts for journaling opportunities.

While some of you may find journaling to come naturally, for others journaling is the more difficult piece of a devotional time. I personally struggled to maintain a consistent journal, especially during the time we worked through the adoption. Looking back now, I wish I had been more faithful in writing down the joys and frustrations, my intimate thoughts and desires, and all the twists and turns we took along the way. Why? As adoptive parents, we are likely to not have photographs of growing, pregnant bellies and prenatal ultrasounds to look back on after a child has been welcomed into our lives. However, through journaling, you can preserve the most intimate thoughts and prayers during this time in your life, perhaps some of which you may even want to share with your children as they grow up.

I want to finally encourage you to move through these devotions at a pace that is right for you. I know that your agenda can be crowded with other obligations, especially as you prepare to grow your family through adoption. The conversations you have allowed me to share with you through this devotional should not be a burden added to an already crazy schedule. I will encourage you to be intentional in spending time with God throughout each day and each step of the process, whether this devotional is a part of that time with God or not. Establishing a lifestyle that incorporates regular, intimate time alone with your Heavenly Father will only serve to strengthen your faith and secure the most stable relationship with God.

Dear friend, I promise you that once that precious little one is in your care, life will take on a whole new, exciting, wonderful, crazy, unbelievable, and totally unexpected form and fashion! Your life, through adoption, becomes a living testimony of the greatness of God's love for each of us. You will touch lives of people you will never know. And in the creation of your new family, I'll be struggling to contain my smile and tears of joy for you!

## Adoption Timeline

Inspiration to adopt: _____

Decision to adopt: _____

Filed the adoption application: _____

Began the homestudy: _____

Submitted the homestudy: _____

Received referral of our child: _____

Saw our child's picture for the first time: _____

Formally accepted the referral: _____

First time meeting our child: _____

First meal together: _____

Received the court date: _____

Initial court appearance: _____

First night together: _____

Final court appearance: _____

Additional important dates: _____

_____

_____

_____

_____

_____

*Date:*_____

## Spirit of Adoption

## Romans 8:15-27

*The Spirit himself testifies with our spirit that we are God's children.*
Romans 8:16

Present day uses of the term *adoption* tend to take away from the significance of the spiritual roots of true adoption. One can clean up trash from the roadway and claim to have "adopted it," people "adopt" animals as pets regularly, and for a few dollars one can even "adopt" a star in outer space. But the permanent adoption of a child into your family is far different and presents a beautiful, tangible picture of our adoption into God's family.

Some thousands of years ago our family tree was broken away from the perfectly designed relationship with God that He intended for us in our creation. We were literally orphaned from God because of a decision in the Garden. When you consider the state of our fallen world, separated from God, imagine the similarities for orphans who live their lives without mothers or fathers. Who do they look up to in their times of distress? Who is their comforter? Who is a trusted advisor? Where is their hope of inheritance? When you consider these questions, there is a large consuming void where loving answers should be. Our human condition, short of adoption through God's love, is even more bleak than that of an orphan.

God's love for us is so great that He has offered each of us the gift of adoption. God's adoption plan is far from the trivial uses of the word "adoption" mentioned previously. It is even greater than the earthly process of adopting an orphan in despair. God's adoption has freed us from slavery to death. Heavenly adoption makes us sons and daughters of God. Receiving God's adoption includes an inheritance shared with Christ. God's adoption plan for us included intense love and sacrifice.

Does any of this sound similar to the adoption your family is pursuing? There is a child desperately desiring to be rescued from a lifetime of separation from a loving family. Through love, dedication, and sacrifice, you are making a way for this child to be legally and intimately included in your family, calling you mother, or father. Adoption means that they will be fully your child, with every privilege a naturally born child would anticipate. They can have hope for a future.

Through earthly adoption, you are being given a gift, not just the gift of a child to love and raise, but the gift of having a deeper, more intimate understanding of your own heavenly adoption.

*Journal*

Consider the parallels between the human separation from God as Father and the child you seek to adopt. Identifying moments of loss, hope, love, sacrifice, and inheritance in both situations will strengthen your relationship with your Heavenly Father, as well as strengthen your ability to love and nourish the intimacy between you and your child.

## Journal continued

## Prayer

*Abba, Father, thank you for adopting me. Continue to increase my insight about Your love for me through our family's adoption. Amen.*

*Date:*_____

## GREATER THAN YOU CAN COUNT

## GENESIS 15:1-6

*Look up in the sky and count the stars – if indeed you can count them… so shall your offspring be.*
                                                    Genesis 15:5

Abraham and his wife, Sarah, were hoping for a miracle. They longed for children of their own, but the reality of their age was working against them. There was an impending sense of urgency, so much so that they fell into the temptation of trying to create their own desired outcome instead of waiting on what God had planned for them. While God's plan was to bless Abraham and his wife with their own biological children, adoption is certainly within God's design as well. The problem was in Abraham and Sarah's impatience, not God's provision and plan.

A desire to grow your family through adoption is a fire that is burning within you. Why does it take so long and why are there so many obstacles? So many children need a home and a family, and you are ready and eagerly willing to open your hearts and home to a child, yet you find yourself having to wait. Some days it likely feels as if there is no end to the waiting and you may begin to wonder if your miracle – and your child's miracle – will ever come through.

God is working out His plan in your life and your child's life. Do not give up. Don't take a seemingly easy route or shortcut. Do not try to script God's plan. Let it happen in His timing. Anything you try to push through or advance out of God's design and plan will eventually only lead to heartbreak.

The day will come when your family's adoption is realized. The hopes and dreams of an orphan will be lived out in your adoption of this child. Your hopes and dreams will be fulfilled. Your faithfulness while enduring a time of waiting will be rewarded through a loving relationship with this child in your life. The blessing you will each receive in your lives as a result of your faith, patience, and perseverance while trusting in God's promise will be far greater than anything you could ever hope or imagine – more than the stars in the sky.

*Journal*

Are there temptations that are drawing your attention away from the adoption promises God has placed in your life? Are there obstacles that seem so great that they might never be overcome? What are your hopes and dreams that only God can fulfill through the adoption of your child? Be courageous in committing these things to paper and then reflect on them as a way to guide your prayer time. When you recognize both the promises and the temptations, you are in a better position to avoid one and receive the other.

___

*Prayer*

*All powerful God, you know the desire of our family's heart. We long for the child You have chosen for us to be living in our home and family so that we can share with him/her the same love that You have for us. Help us to be patient and wait for your perfect timing. Protect us from the temptation to stray outside of Your awesome plan. Thank you for the blessings You are pouring out on our lives, so many and so great that they are beyond our wildest imagination! Amen.*

Date:_____

## ENTRUSTED TO YOUR CARE

## 1 SAMUEL 21:10 - 22:5

*From there David went to Mizpah in Moab and said to the king of Moab, "would you let my father and mother come and stay with you until I learn what God will do for me?"*
1 Samuel 22:3

David was fleeing the wrath of Saul when he recognized that he was no longer in a position to care for his family. In a very dark and painful, even fearful time in David's life, he had to make a hard decision – to trust his beloved family to the care of another.

As you work through mountains of red tape and paperwork, likely with the prayers of friends and family supporting you in the long and often tedious process filled with uncertainties and frustrations, take some time to lift up in prayer the mother and father who have been confronted with separation from their child. Just as David was eagerly awaiting God's provision for his life, these families are seeking what God has for their children as well.

David was not haphazard in selecting the one who would

care for his family and was thoughtful in selecting the king of Moab to entrust with his family's well-being. Just as David vetted the king for this enormous task, you too are being examined for your ability to raise another's beloved child. As you work to meet the legal requirements for adoption, consider the additional aspects of your faith which hold you to a higher level of accountability to God. God is interested in maturing you into the family who is fit for the important job ahead.

*Journal*

In which areas of your life do you need specific prayer and guidance that will allow you to grow into the best family possible to care for someone else's child? Allow yourself to be vulnerable as you write these down and consider sharing them with your closest prayer warriors.

_____

_____

_____

_____

_____

## 24 | Open Hearts

*Journal continued*

_____

_____

_____

_____

_____

_____

_____

_____

_____

_____

*Prayer*

*Heavenly father, bless the birth family of my children during their time of difficulty. Help me to be in the best position to care for these precious children who will soon be in our home, lives, and family forever. Amen*

*Date:*_____

## SUSTAINING THE FATHERLESS

## PSALMS 146:1-10

*The Lord watches over the foreigner and sustains the fatherless and the widow, but he frustrates the way of the wicked.*
*Psalm 146:9*

When we learned our youngest was ill and in need of medicine, but 7000 miles away and with limited access to care, it was difficult for us knowing that there was little we could do in person to comfort our little girl. But where we could not provide, God could, and He did. Not only did she receive the treatment she needed, we trusted that God would heal her body and comfort her soul. The Holy Spirit is not bound by government regulations or geographical and political borders.

In this Scripture, the Psalmist is not only offering us hope in God's provision for the fatherless, but is also offering praise to God for the help He provides. This psalm begins and ends with a declaration of praise to the Lord, with a number of the reasons for such praise sandwiched in between. The psalmist is asking you to trust in the Lord alongside him and offer your own praise for the protection and provision God provides.

As a parent, you want to be able to hold your child, reassure them, and comfort them whether they are sick, afraid, or feeling alone. At this stage in your adoption journey, you may not yet be able to have this kind of intimate and loving contact with your child. As you confront the knowledge that your future son or daughter is alive and right now facing the struggles of life somewhere beyond where you can currently reach them, comfort them, and protect them, remember that they are being sustained by their heavenly Father.

Learning to trust your child to God at this early stage will benefit you in the years of parenting to come. You won't always be able to be physically present for your child, and will often be forced to rely on the upbringing you have given them and the protection of their Father in Heaven.

*Journal*

What concerns for your child do you have when you think about this time when you are apart from him/her? As you journal, consider the fears that you have as well as the struggles your child might have as you are apart. Use these concerns to guide your prayer, for your own peace and the protection for your child that only God can give.

*Journal continued*

_____

_____

_____

_____

_____

_____

_____

_____

*Prayer*

*I praise You, God, for all that You are doing to protect and sustain my child during this time that we are so far apart. You are powerful to provide in ways beyond my abilities and so good to be the help and hope for our family. Help me to trust in Your goodness now and even more as our family grows. Praise the Lord!*

Date:_____

## UP AGAINST AN ARMY

## 2 CHRONICLES 20:1-30

*"Do not be afraid or discouraged because of this vast army. For the battle is not yours, but God's."*
*—Spirit of the Lord*
2 Chronicles 20:15b

Is the agency going to approve our home study? Will we be able to carry the financial requirements of the adoption? What will be the final court ruling? When will our child be able to come home with us? The list of potential sources of anxiety can seem endless. This adoption is a major adjustment in your family's future and the effects of such a major change can naturally cause a degree of stress.

Jehoshaphat was a God-loving king of Judah in the Old Testament. A time came when he faced a major threat to his life and the lives of the people he led. Jehoshaphat was up against a vast army and the intense reality of the situation rightly caused him genuine alarm (v. 3). Feeling the strain of stress and anxiety, he and the people openly sought God's assistance. Read Jehoshaphat's cry to God in verses 6-12 again. Do you hear the anxiety, the stress fueled desperation, uncertainty and fear? He concludes with an admission that he does not know what to do but is seeking God for an answer.

Jehoshaphat and the people – men, wives, and children – made their earnest plea and then they stood before God, faithfully waiting for an answer. They didn't try to attend to the impending crisis on their own or continue to fret in their natural anxiety. The king and the families of the kingdom waited for a reply from God.

Always faithful, the Spirit of the Lord first gave them hope and comfort to ease their hearts and minds (v. 15). The Spirit then gave the people direction for the action they could take to be successful (v. 16-17). He gave them hope and resources – the same thing He offers us.

Hope is an excellent remedy for anxiety. The hope God gave to the king, men, women, and children of Judah is the same hope available to your family in every stressful situation you encounter along this adoption journey. When you feel like you are facing an army, look to God to carry you through to victory.

*Journal*

Consider the things that are causing anxiety in your life now. What about the others in your family who are being impacted by the adoption journey? What are the fears and vast armies that you face as you move forward in the adoption? Take these concerns to God as a family. Then wait for the Spirit of the Lord to answer. He will!

_____

_____

_____

_____

_____

_____

_____

_____

_____

_____

*Prayer*

*Mighty and powerful God, our family stands before you today with anxieties about the process of adoption. We give these over to you and praise You as we seek the comfort only You can give. Show us the battle plan and guide us forward. Amen.*

Date:_____

## PATIENT OR PLEADING

## MARK 5:21-42

*Ignoring what they said, Jesus told the synagogue ruler, "Don't be afraid; just believe."*

Mark 5:36

Our family's adoption journey was requiring an increasingly greater amount of energy to continue to remain patient in a process that seems to be moving slower than naturally possible and dragging on inexplicably longer than anticipated. We reached times when we almost dreaded occasions when friends would ask about the progress of the adoption because it seemed like there was all too often nothing new to report. *No, there was no real update, just the same waiting*, we would explain while trying to remain cheerful. I began to think people were secretly questioning if our family's adoption would ever be realized, and I sometimes began to wonder this myself.

Jarius, a ruler in the synagogue, sought Jesus for the healing of his dying daughter. He was not asking meekly and patiently, Jarius was on the ground pleading earnestly. Jesus could have certainly restored the girl in an instant, but instead he made his way through the crowd and performed other miracles while on the way to Jarius' home (v. 22-23). Before reaching the girl, some friends came to Jarius and Jesus and told them to stop being concerned over the girl, it was too late, she had already died (v. 35). But reading on we know that this was not a concern for Jesus; He wasn't discouraged because of a bad report. He knew the plan was to restore the girl, even from what appeared to be the most hopeless of situations: her death.

Instead of being discouraged, or talking about how big the obstacles are, or repetitively surveying the odds that your adoption will come through, consider this: Well before you even considered taking those initial steps into the adoption process, God was already at work shaping a path for your family to grow through this adoption. Take comfort in knowing that God has worked innumerable miracles throughout history and He is still the God of miracles today. Do not let the appearance of inactivity allow discouragement to settle in. You are fulfilling a piece of God's ministry purpose for your family's life through adoption and He will be faithful in making a way even when all outward appearances indicate that you should be discouraged.

*Journal*

What are some of the sources of discouragement you are facing? Acknowledge the frustrations and then draw a line through each of them, writing instead the promises of God and the reasons for your faith and hope.

_____

_____

_____

_____

_____

_____

_____

_____

*Prayer*

*Father God, I offer you my praise for the miracle you are working in our lives right now, and I am believing in faith for the good report and positive outcome in our adoption process. Despite the reports that might try to discourage, our family is holding on to our trust that you are Almighty God and that You are working in the places we cannot see right now so that our child no longer will live as an orphan. Thank you for growing us in our faith. Amen.*

Date:_____

## A LOVE QUESTION

## 1 JOHN 4:7-21

*If anyone acknowledges that Jesus is the Son of God, God lives in him and he in God.*
1 John 4:15

A worry once seldom mentioned but receiving growing attention is the concern of adoptive parents that they will not feel a strong sense of connection and love for their adopted children. Sometimes associated with this worry are issues such as a lack of healthy attachment in the children or post-adoption depression in parents, which is compounded by the normal stresses of adoptive parenthood.

God is love. Pure, unadulterated, steadfast, eternal, unconditional love. His is a love so great that our worst moments can be forgiven and erased in an instant. It is that love that facilitated your adoption by a Heavenly Father. At the point when you were adopted, God began living inside you and became the source of your ability to love others. Without God, a person is left to their own feeble resources to conjure up a counterfeit version of love, one that is susceptible to doubt, envy, distrust, and eventually failure.

Much of the research focused on attachment topic comes from the secular perspective on adoption. Perhaps there is some cause to be concerned that parents might not have the capacity to feel love for their adopted children, especially considering that the source of true love is not present in the lives of non-Believers. But as a Christian, there is a Holy Spirit presence in your life which adds a new source of love, having a very real impact on your life and your ability to love your children.

As you push forward in your adoption journey, meditate on the goodness of God's love in your life. God's perfect love is patient, kind, truthful, forgiving, protecting, hopeful, persevering, and unfailing (1 Corinthians 13:4-8). As your sensitivity to God's love for you deepens, so too will be your ability to share that love with others, including your child.

*Journal*

Openly and honestly acknowledging God's love for you is the first step in deepening your true love relationships with others. In your journal, complete the following statement:

I know of God's love for me because…

---

---

*Journal continued*

_____

_____

_____

_____

_____

_____

_____

_____

_____

*Prayer*

*Heavenly Father, thank you for loving me beyond all my imperfections. I am so grateful for the Holy Spirit living in me, who is the source of my love. I want to experience more of your love in my life so that I can share Your love with everyone I meet, and especially with the child you are bringing into our family. I love you, God. Amen.*

*Date:*_____

## CONSTRUCTION PROCESS

## GENESIS 6:8-22

*This is how you build it: The ark is to be three hundred cubits long, fifty cubits wide and thirty cubits high.*
Genesis 6:15

The number of certified forms, official copies, and notarized signatures can be overwhelming at times during this process, which may seem to be moving at an incredibly slow pace. You have likely already put in some long hours chasing down all the required documents, getting certified copies, making countless trips to the notary public, and maintaining at least a semi-organized file of your progress. While you may have many supportive people in your circle of influence, when it comes to the actual process of doing the hard, meticulous work of pre-adoption, you are the one who has to carry the load and put in the sweat. Meanwhile, you may pass Mother's and Father's Day celebrations without your child, forego family vacations while others enjoy such trips, or spend restless nights wondering how all the effort and sacrifice could ever eventually lead to your adoption.

Noah was faced with a similar challenge when God

instructed him to build an ark. To build a 450 foot long ship with little earthly assistance while the rest of the world was zipping along merrily with their lives must have certainly been frustrating for Noah. But he knew that at the end of his hard work, his family would eternally benefit from his obedience, hard work and sacrifice. We don't know for sure when he began the work on the ark, but he was 600 years old when it was finished. When the rain came, his effort was rewarded with his family's new start in a renewed world.

The task of processing the legal requirements for an adoption is demanding, tiresome, stressful, and requires a great deal of sacrifice and an enduring commitment. We know that Noah walked with God before he began the process of building the ark (v. 9) and we can trust that Noah continued his close connection with God throughout the construction process. Be encouraged by Noah's constant walk with God as you build your adoption dossier. In the end of the "building process" the reward for your faithfulness will be great!

*Journal*

You have likely made numerous lists of the tasks that need to be completed in various stages of the adoption process. Now, how about considering the intentional time you are taking with God? Create a plan for the things you are going to do to strengthen your walk with God. Make a list. Be specific. Ask God to help you see the areas which need strengthened right now. Review this list and then put it into action. Treat this plan with at least the same intensity that you address the adoption demands.

_____

_____

_____

_____

_____

_____

_____

_____

_____

*Prayer*

*Lord God, help me to stay focused on the plan you have for our family. I believe You have given us an amazing opportunity to receive Your blessing. You know how difficult this process can be at times so I am asking for Your strength, guidance and wisdom as we push through this phase of the adoption. As we proceed, my heart is overjoyed with the knowledge of the blessings to come. Amen.*

Date:_____

## WILL YOU LOVE ME?

## EPHESIANS 3:14-21

*Then Christ will make his home in your hearts as you trust in him. Your roots will grow down into God's love and keep you strong.*
Ephesians 3:17 (NLT)

Early in any adoption process, prospective parents are often educated about the possibility of adopted children having difficulties forming healthy attachment patterns with their adoptive family. Since such struggles can be real, don't be surprised if the enemy doesn't try to get the idea in your head that your child might not attach with you and love you as a parent. What if they don't love me? Why won't they trust? Cuddle? Make eye contact? Why do they not care if I'm in the room? These are natural worries of many prospective adopting families.

Your child will meet you as a stranger. They rely on their previous experiences with others to assess you. These past experiences might include disappointment, betrayal, abuse, pain, neglect, or abandonment. Your child will assess you through your interactions to determine when it is safe to be more affectionate, less guarded, and more trusting. Different children, coming from different past experiences and with their own unique personalities, will react at a different pace. It is our task, as adoptive parents, to be consistent in our love with our children, while relying on God's movement in their hearts and minds. Consistent love makes the way for them to grow and know you as their loving and trusted parent.

When you first came to know Jesus, your perception of Him was based on your past experiences. It was a brand new relationship in which you were just beginning to learn the depth of the intimacy of your relationship and God's love. Over time, your relationship matures and deepens with God as your Heavenly parent because of the time you spend together and the trust built as He continues to care for you.

As you show a lasting and gentle love to your child, he/she will also learn to grow closer to you. Just like when there may be times that you are hesitant to believe that God could really care for you in your early relationship with Him, your child will recall the times that they were afraid to trust because of the times they had been disappointed before. Consistent love and nurturing will strengthen the relationship and help your child to grow their love for you as their mother or father.

*Journal*

What was your first perception of God? How has that changed over time? What things caused that to change?

How can you use this reflection to nourish a loving relationship with your child?

_____

_____

_____

_____

_____

_____

_____

_____

_____

*Prayer*

*Father, thank you for Your patience and consistent love for me. Help me to show the same love and nurturing for the child You have chosen for our family. Comfort this child's heart and mind as he/she learns to know me as mother or father.*

*Date:*_____

## FIGHTING TWO BATTLES

## 1 JOHN 2:15-17

*The world and its desires pass away, but whoever does the will of God lives forever.*
1 John 2:17

The days will draw out to a time when it may seem like there is no progress being made in your case and the adoption process is stuck on pause. There is nothing you can do in the earthly process but wait – no form you can submit or phone call that can be made to get things moving along. It may appear that the entire adoption process has come to a grinding halt.

Caring for orphans in their distress is one of God's charges for Believers and you are carrying out the will of the heart of God by adopting. You are, by that virtue, not only engaging in natural battles of bureaucracy and regulations, but also a spiritual battle. The enemy doesn't want you to be successful and would be thrilled if you ignored the spiritual element in this stage of your life. While the natural battle may be easier to see and feel right now, the spiritual one is the greater battle.

Sooner or later, there will be visible progress (perhaps happening at a rate that will make your head spin!), the adoption will come through and these legal struggles will be a thing of the past. And eventually, your children will grow up, mature, leave home and start their own families. Eventually we will age and pass on to the next life. Eventually, all the things of this earth will pass and all that will matter is what has been accomplished in the spiritual realm. So consider the importance of the spiritual battle going on right now. When it seems like all you can do is wait, remember that there is always a spiritual battle waging on. Pray, study, love each other, connect with spiritual encouragers, grow your faith, and continually train to overcome obstacles for the glory of God.

## *Journal*

How do you perceive God's plan of love being carried out in your family's adoption? What are some areas where you can benefit from spiritual growth while you work toward the completion of the adoption? Are there tangible steps you can take to strengthen your relationship with God? How will you use the "down time" in the adoption process to invest in your family's spiritual future?

_____

_____

_____

## 45 | Waiting Homes

*Journal continued*

*Prayer*

*God, show me how to grow spiritually during this time so that I can be victorious in the earthly battles as well as in the eternally important spiritual battles. Amen.*

Date:_____

## COMPASSION IN DISTRESS

## JAMES 1:19-27

*Religion that God our Father accepts as pure and faultless is this: to look after orphans and widows in their distress…"*
*James 1:27*

James was writing to the church, offering encouragement and direction regarding some of the "bigger picture" of Christian living and behavior. Within the instruction James presents, those of us who have had our lives touched with adoption are likely to be especially sensitive to the instruction to "look after orphans in their distress" (v. 27). James provides this action as an example of religion that is pure, without fault, and an important act of Christian compassion ordained by God.

Adoption is certainly a beautiful act of love, but let's consider for a moment the issue James touches on when it comes to orphans – their distress. Our own family's adoption pictures are filled with images of true love. But the backstory for children without their birth families is wrought with distress. Experiencing the death of parents, nightmarish family histories, abuse, uncertainty, and so forth are often fresh on the hearts and minds of children who may become available for adoption into a loving and stable home. In short, the path that your children are traveling to reach your home and family might not fit the definition of "beautiful" which is so often used to describe an adoption.

When I first met our girls in a sub-Saharan African orphanage, I was overjoyed and literally speechless with love and excitement. But from our girls' perspective, I was a stranger who was whisking them away from the last fragments of anything they found familiar. I can't know exactly their thoughts, but their body language confirmed that they were cautious, suspicious, and sometimes afraid. From their perspective, this was not a time of celebration but a time of uncertainty and fear which was based largely on their distress-filled past experiences. It took consistent love, gentle encouragement, and time to convince them that this new direction in their lives was going to be a great one.

So while you should eagerly anticipate this child coming into your life, be cautious not to ignore the distress endured or suffered by your child and selfishly only focus on the wondrous fulfillment of *your* adoption dream. Take the time to be sensitive to the traumatic experiences which brought your child to the loving embrace of their new family.

*Journal*

Planning the welcome home or "gotcha day" celebrations is a time each adoptive family looks forward to with eager anticipation. What plans have you made for your child's homecoming? What measures can you take to ensure they are protected from additional stressors? How can you plan now to be sensitive to the distressful past your child has experienced?

_____

_____

_____

_____

_____

_____

_____

_____

_____

_____

*Journal continued*

_____

_____

_____

_____

_____

_____

_____

*Prayer*

*Father, comfort the child you are placing in our home. Calm their thoughts and ease their minds. Help me to be sensitive to their needs which has resulted from the distress they have endured. Amen.*

Date:_____

## You've Been Sent

## Judges 6:7-16

*The Lord turned to him and said, "Go in the strength you have and save Israel out of Midian's hand. Am I not sending you?"*
Judges 6:14

During this time of working toward your adoption, don't be surprised if your ears and mind are finely tuned to pick up on any news of other adoption stories. Whether it is yet another celebrity who is showcasing a seemingly painless and near perfect story of adoption which appears to have been realized overnight with the same magic used in the movies, or it is the story of a friend or acquaintance who tells of the beautiful moments of an adoption story they know of, you'll likely reach a point in which you feel your adoption process is one wrought with setbacks, impossibilities, and frustrations. The most well-meaning folks will share wondrous adoption stories, and they will be inspiring to hear, but when you sit with the long lists of requirements, rearrange your finances once again to fulfill yet another payment, and wait for days, weeks, months or years for your family's adoption to be realized, it may feel at times more hopeless than miraculous.

Gideon felt much the same when he was called out by God to stand up against a mighty invading army. He was not entirely convinced that he could complete the task God had appointed him to carry out. Gideon compared himself to others who appeared to be much more capable or successful. But God reminded Gideon that he would not be alone in this battle, that He would strengthen Gideon for the task at hand, and that he would succeed. If you read on and follow the story through chapter 7, not only did Gideon succeed in battle but he did so with fewer resources than seemingly necessary. Gideon accomplished the task at hand with God's strength.

So I encourage you to lift up weary eyes when the mounting requirements for the completion of your family's adoption seem to overwhelm your resources and abilities. God calls us to look after orphans in their distress, and your family's adoption is a beautiful reflection of our spiritual adoption into God's eternal family. When God is calling you to open your heart and home to the children He has planned for you, He will strengthen you to succeed in the endeavor.

*Journal*

What are the specific struggles you are facing right now that are causing concern or stress in your family's adoption process? Take the time to write them out. Then present these concerns to God. Tell Him all the areas where you are struggling or fearful. (He already knows about them but it makes a difference when you sit with God and tell Him yourself). At the end of this list, write out the response God gave to Gideon in Verse 14.

_____

_____

_____

_____

_____

_____

_____

_____

*Prayer*

*Help me, God, to be strong. This is often a difficult journey and ministry to which You have called me. Strengthen me and help me to keep focused on the prize! Amen.*

Date:_____

## GROWING THE HEART AND HEAD

## PROVERBS 19:2

*Desire without knowledge is not good — how much more will hasty feet miss the way!*
                                                                Proverbs 19:2

You don't need to be reminded that the process of adoption is a long and tedious journey with countless officials wanting to know some of the more intimate details of your life. It is natural to want the process to happen faster while the issues that seem to bring the whole thing to a grandly slow pace often seem inexplicably absurd – take a class, fill out more forms, wait for appointments, do it all over again, update this and that. It seems that there is always someone wanting more information before they will put their seal of approval on your case. It can be utterly frustrating when your ultimate heart's desire is to fill a special place you have created in your home and heart through a loving adoption.

I encourage you to take this time, when the pace is slow, to expand your own knowledge. While the investigation or search for information into your case and your life continues, grow your own knowledge about adoption and the unique struggles of bringing a child into your family. Look for areas where fresh wisdom will benefit you such as family finances, scheduling for a new lifestyle, fostering attachment, and understanding the culture to which your child has been accustomed.

This learning process need not always be technical or hardcore. Make it enjoyable! Our daughter's lived their first few years enjoying traditional African meals. Accepting that a great way to bond with our children was through food, I learned to cook a few of their favorite dishes. From steamed plantains to "goat-on-a-stick," our family still enjoys some of the tastes of our daughters' birth country.

*Journal*

What are some specific areas where you need more information that will benefit your family's future? What steps can you take to seek out this knowledge?

_____

_____

_____

_____

_____

*Journal continued*

_____
_____
_____
_____
_____
_____
_____
_____

*Prayer*

*Oh Lord, I confess that there is so much I do not know. I am boldly asking for your wisdom as the time becomes closer that I will be the appointed earthly parent for the child(ren) You are placing in my care. Show me the areas I need to grow my knowledge and fill me with eager anticipation to learn all that You would have me know to be the best parent I can possibly be. Amen.*

Date:_____

## Time to Celebrate

## Luke 15:11-24

*Let's have a feast and celebrate.*
Luke 15:22

In the parable of the lost son, the father was overjoyed that his son was coming home, despite the less than honorable way he had lived his life and squandered his inheritance. An alternative reaction could have been more like the other sons, who were irritated at the celebration. We could speculate other possible outcomes including approaching the son with concern, suspicion and caution about the motivation for the son's return, or feelings of shame because of his choices and lifestyle. Instead of these potential responses, the father orchestrated a massive celebration.

Our family had a long wait for the first of several appointments with the U.S. Embassy in our child's birth country. I was sweat-soaked from the equatorial African heat and humidity, covered in reddish dust from the dirt road after a kilometer walk to get bottled water, and long desiring some of the creature comforts of home when the call finally came. We had been granted an appointment at the Embassy the next morning! Despite still facing a number of hurdles in-country, news of this small step was cause for celebration! We cheered and danced!

When the struggles of adoption yield more delays and frustrations than the eagerly anticipated news that your child will be home with you soon, it is important to shift your attitude to one of celebration. Look for opportunities to celebrate. No step in the process is too small or insignificant. That email which confirmed receipt of another document means you are a step closer – celebrate. The request for more information means your case is getting attention – celebrate. And yes, even when you face delays you can find peace and celebrate a God who is guiding your steps and preparing the perfect way for your family, so celebrate.

*Journal*

What are the events that you have cause to celebrate right now? Think back and recognize some seemingly small or even the big steps forward in your case, perhaps some that you overlooked or simply acknowledged as not a big deal. What are some upcoming events in which you can find cause to celebrate? Write them out and have some intentional celebration!

*Journal continued*

_____
_____
_____
_____
_____
_____
_____
_____
_____
_____

*Prayer*

*Father, show me all the reasons to celebrate along this adoption journey. Don't allow discouragement to settle in or frustration rule my perspective. Help me keep my focus on the positive aspects of each step in this journey.*

Date:_____

## HARD CHOICES

## PHILIPPIANS 1:9-11

*And this is my prayer: that your love may abound more and more in knowledge and depth of insight.*
Philippians 1:9

The time will come when a referral for a child awaiting adoption will be placed in front of you. You'll have a brief glimpse into this child's life and have to make a decision. Will you be the parent this child desperately needs? Or is there an issue that causes you so much concern that you are wary of accepting the referral of this child? Whether the decision comes easily or with great difficulty, a choice still has to be made whether or not you will accept for all eternity this child who is being offered to you.

You'll have to consider your family's position and the reports given to you by the agency. Is the child healthy and well or are there known medical issues? What about all the unknowns? It is likely that there is far more you won't know than what you do know about the child's history. This is a time when the ability to use spiritual discernment will be so vitally important.

After enduring the heartbreak of losing the first little girl who we planned to adopt, our family offered to God that would wait patiently for the child He planned to have in our home. Within a few months, we received a call from our agency. "How about sisters?," they asked, even though we had planned for only one child. In my heart I knew that these were the children God intended for us to adopt. When we were later told that one child was potentially significantly disabled, it was not hard to reply with, "that is ok with us, she is our daughter whom God has designated for our family!"

So how do you grow your spiritual discernment? Pray, study God's word, get wise counsel from those you trust, and then be still enough to listen to the Holy Spirit directing your path. As a parent especially, but also for your life in general, you will benefit from an ongoing nurturing of your spiritual discernment abilities. Which school will she go to? Is this boy okay to date? Do I punish or show mercy? You have to discern.

What is the Holy Spirit telling you about the child you are adopting? What about all the other steps involved in this process? Do you take out a loan or ask for donations to finance your adoption, or is a temporary second income in order? Some other things are likely without question. Will your child attend church with you? Will you raise them up in a Godly faith. Undoubtedly every aspect of life requires discernment, and this is especially true of your family's adoption. It is never too soon to grow your spiritual discernment skills and you will never be so mature that there is no longer a need to strengthen spiritual discernment.

*Journal*

What are some of the questions you have that require a higher level of spiritual discernment? What are some resources you can implement beginning right now to grow your discernment?

_____

_____

_____

_____

_____

_____

_____

_____

_____

_____

*Journal continued*

_____

_____

_____

_____

_____

_____

*Prayer*

*God, I want to know what path you desire for me. In the largest and the smallest decisions, I desire to be walking in Your will. Help me to grow in my ability to hear the Holy Spirit speak to me and guide me, especially in our family's adoption process. Amen.*

Date:_____

## BRINGING DOWN THE WALLS

## JOSHUA 5:13 – 6:21

*The seventh time around, when the priests sounded the trumpet blast, Joshua commanded the army, "Shout! For the Lord has given you the city!*
Joshua 6:16

Not once around Jericho but seven times marching and playing instruments. Those tactics are not the skills you normally would expect to bring a wall crashing down. It is estimated that the combination of walls surrounding Jericho were up to 46 feet above ground level and 6 feet thick. It surrounded a city of around 6 acres. It was a tremendous obstacle. Walking around it playing music wouldn't seem like the best way to achieve victory. But that was exactly the process prescribed.

One of the steps in our family's adoption involved joining a tribe in Africa. Though more a formality than anything, it did require a day trip to the King's office while in-country, selection of a suitable tribe, and learning a little of the local language. It was an unexpected and quite unusual part of the adoption process, and one that was not easy for a foreigner such as myself to navigate. But I trusted in God and the people He placed in my life at that point in the process to get us through it successfully. In the end, I joined the *Ngo* tribe and that piece of the adoption puzzle makes for interesting conversation now.

The adoption process can seem as much a challenge as the wall around Jericho. With so many children around the world in desperate need of loving families, some of the requirements to complete an adoption can seem trivial and an absurd exercise in redundancy. Some of the tasks you have to complete, and often repeat, may seem as unusual as singing around a wall to conquer a city. But that is the process that has been required.

Joshua trusted God's unusual instructions for leading his army to victory at Jericho. Perseverance and following the prescribed guidance got the job done and the work was rewarded. You'll likely face a number of unusual or frustrating requests throughout your adoption journey. Approach each one with God's wisdom and direction and you will attain the goal!

*Journal*

Recall some of the unusual requests that have been asked of you so far. What are the frustrations you face which seem to hinder your progress in completing the adoption? What is your plan for approaching the obstacles that seem to slow your adoption process?

___

*Prayer*

*Father, help us to see the obstacles in the way of our adoption as opportunities for You to show Your power and glory. Help me to be obedient and approach these barriers and requirements with the loving patience and depth of discernment that You require. Amen.*

Date:_____

## BIRTH FAMILY FEARS

## GENESIS 43:19-34

*When portions were served to them from Joseph's table, Benjamin's portion was five times as much as anyone else's. So they feasted and drank freely with him.*
                                                                Genesis 43:34

   Many families have concerns about the influence or contact the birth family may have in their child's life now and as they get older. The list can be daunting and will vary depending on your adoption situation. Will there be contact with the birth family? Will your children want to contact their birth family when they are older? How will your children's cultural influence before their adoption impact their interactions with a new family?

   Joseph was sold by his brothers as a young man, but then years later he helped them when they were devastated by famine and desperation. Joseph did not forsake his birth family in retaliation for the trauma he endured at their hands. Despite the negative influence of Joseph's birth family in his younger years, he remembered them in their distress. Joseph provided for them out of the abundance he possessed from his new life.

When you consider the situation of a birth family, it is not possible to dismiss their impact on your child. Two people created this child and a mother birthed him/her into this world. Without your child's birth family, he/she would have never taken a single breath in this world.

For some parents, the degree to which they tell a child about their story of adoption will vary and others might consider not disclosing this information at all. While this is a decision your family will have to prayerfully consider, don't discount the role the birth family played in bringing your child to life and the path your child traveled to reach his/her home with your family. Further consider the greater plan God might have for your child, your family, their birth family, and numerous others you will impact as your family grows through adoption.

As you consider the impact a birth family might have on your family's adoption, also give thought to the impact you can have on them. Joseph had been blessed by God and he shared this blessing with the very people who sold him into slavery. As you raise your child, the Godly love you impart in their life can have a tremendous influence on the impact your child can have on others.

## Journal

What examples do you want to set in your child's life? How will the example they see in you have an impact on the ways they can then influence others, including the family or culture into which they were birthed?

_____

_____

_____

_____

_____

_____

_____

_____

_____

## Prayer

*Father, give me the wisdom to know how to approach my child's birth family. Instead of fear or hesitation, help me to see the wondrous ways we can be a blessing to them through this adoption. Amen.*

Date:_____

# HEARTBREAK AND HOPE

# GENESIS 4:8-26

*"God has granted me another child in place of Abel, since Cain killed him."*
Genesis 4:25b

I cannot imagine the pain that Eve suffered when she learned that one of her sons had murdered the other. After carrying these children in her womb while struggling to work the ground, find a place to sleep at night, live in the world now separated from a once perfect relationship with God and then enduring the agony of childbirth, she now faced the death of one at the hands of the other, who himself was now banished.

As our family was mentally preparing to travel overseas to meet a child we hoped would soon be our daughter, we received the unexpected and devastating news that the government of her birth country decided to cease current and future adoptions of her type to the United States. We were devastated. This little girl whom we had grown to love through a small photograph was being ripped from our hearts and home. The adoption agency simply referred to this as an "interruption." For our family, it seemed that the long journey to adopting a child had come to an end and we mourned as if we had lost a child to death. What adoption agencies refer to simply as "interruptions" can be minor delays or gut-wrenching losses.

As prospective adoptive families progress through the hurdles of adoption, it is an ever-present reality that a heartbreaking setback can occur. But we proceed through the process anyway, fueled by hope and carried by faith. When confronted with setbacks or disasters in the process, it is perfectly acceptable to grieve the loss that has been experienced. The loss of a disrupted adoption can be as devastating as that suffered by Eve in the death of one son and the loss of contact with the other son.

No matter the hurts she endured, Eve did not dwell in her pain. She continued on and was later blessed with another son, Seth. The first two children born on this earth met tragic fates. The first woman to ever give birth did not let this pain stop her from pushing on and continuing to grow her family. There was no guarantee that this attempt would yield any better results, but that didn't stop her. (If she had given up because it was too difficult, I imagine none of us would be here!) As adoptive families, we can mourn our losses, but must remain hopeful that we will attain the goal of adoption.

## Waiting Homes

*Journal*

Are there setbacks or disappointments you have experienced so far? Has there been a heartbreaking loss? What are your greatest fears when you think of potential adoption problems?

_____

_____

_____

_____

_____

_____

_____

_____

*Prayer*

*God, I trust that caring for orphans in their distress is in Your plan for Believers. Because this is a spiritual battle, I recognize that there may be trials and difficulties along the journey. Help me to keep my hope focused on the goal of bringing a child into our family. Amen.*

Date:_____

## INHERITANCE

## COLOSSIANS 1:1-14

*Giving thanks to the Father, who has qualified you to share in the inheritance of the saints in the kingdom of light.*
Colossians 1:12

When the judge finalizes the order for your family's adoption this little one becomes a lawful member of your family, complete with all the rights that a child born from your flesh and blood would receive. On their own, there is nothing this child could have achieved, accomplished, or strived for which would have allowed this to otherwise occur. It was simply out of their reach. Unattainable by the child except that your dedication, sacrifice, and love coupled with God's providence, accomplished the steps necessary to cause this legal and beautifully binding promise to occur.

We can compare this to the inheritance for which we have been qualified as God's children. It is nothing that we could successfully strive for, work toward, or achieve out of our own power, ability, or shear will. Instead, God our Father qualified each of us to be His children out of His great love for us. Jesus was presented as a sacrifice so that we could each attain sonship to a Heavenly Father through a supernatural adoption.

There was a moment (or more truthfully, several moments!) while I was in Africa when I thought I was way in over my head with our adoption. Our girls had just been allowed to come with me to the temporary housing we arranged while in-country, even though our court date had not yet arrived. In the middle of the night all three of us had a fever with upset stomachs. There was crying, vomiting, and diarrhea, and in a place so foreign to me and out of the reach of any comforts of home, I began to seriously question if I was capable of being a competent parent and still maintain my sanity! Once we had finally settled down on some blankets scattered on the floor near the toilet and the girls were dozing off to sleep, I thought of the sacrifice God made for me, the love He poured out, and the patience He showed me during my good days and especially the rough times. In my journey through an earthly adoption, I began to gain such a greater appreciation of the heavenly adoption I have received!

During this time that you are working toward completion of your family's adoption, there will likely be ups and downs, frustrations and celebrations, overnight happenings and long periods of waiting. God experienced some of the same feelings while waiting on each of us to accept His gift of adoption and inheritance. Recognizing the similarities between our Heavenly adoption and the earthly adoption to which God has called you, there are likely numerous opportunities which will arise that you can benefit from and learn more about your position with Christ as an adopted child of a Heavenly Father.

*Journal*

What have you learned through this adoption that has drawn you into a closer relationship with your Heavenly Father? How can you use this experience to teach your child about their earthly and heavenly adoption?

_____

_____

_____

_____

_____

_____

_____

_____

*Journal continued*

_____

_____

_____

_____

_____

_____

*Prayer*

*Thank you, Father, for loving me enough to make the necessary sacrifice that paved the way for me to be adopted as Your child. Help me to mirror Your love as a parent to this child You are placing in my life. Amen.*

Date:_____

## In Pursuit

## Jeremiah 29:4-14

*You will seek me and find me when you seek me with all your heart.*
                                                                Jeremiah 29:13

When you pursue God, you will find Him. That is a promise you can stand on. Your adoption is full of pursuits also. You have likely ventured on all sorts of mini-pursuits for documents and seal of approvals. All of this has been in the grand pursuit of your child. Completing the necessary requests can become a full-time, or at least a dedicated part-time job and often requires tremendous energy and efforts.

The same is true in our pursuit of God. Time, effort, energy, and sacrifice offered lovingly and passionately are requirements for progress. A passive approach to either God or this adoption will neither bring you the adoption results you desire nor a closer relationship with God.

I had a workstation set up in our home that was dedicated to our adoption. Compete with books full of dog-eared pages covered in highlighted text, checklists and estimated timelines, and organized space to file originals and copies of required documents. I even added a framed photograph our daughters from the referral packet we received. When I sat at the workstation, either to complete more forms or to dream of the day we would finally meet our daughters, any potential distraction was set aside. I wanted to focus solely on the adoption goal. The closer we came to completing the adoption, the easier it was to let the time I spent at our adoption work area consume parts of my life.

Greater than the dedication to pursuing the adoption must be our pursuit of God. It is, after all, God who is guiding the progress of the adoption at every step along the way. When we pursue God with the fervency that we chase down adoption goals, we are permitting Him to be glorified in every aspect of our lives.

*Journal*

What are some areas in which you have pursued and achieved the goal? Are there areas in your life where additional pursuit is warranted? Do you pursue God as fervently as you pursue the adoption requirements?

_____

_____

_____

_____

*Journal continued*

_____
_____
_____
_____
_____
_____
_____
_____
_____

*Prayer*

God, I have dedicated hours, days, weeks, or more to our family's adoption. Help me to maintain a beautiful balance in my life, especially during this time as we prepare our hearts for a child, in which You are the One I pursue with the greatest passion. Amen.

*Date:*_____

## THE MAKING OF A MIRACLE

## MARK 8:22-25

*Once more Jesus put his hand on the man's eyes. Then his eyes were opened, his sight was restored, and he saw everything clearly.*

Mark 8:25

Do you ever wonder what is happening behind the scenes when God is working out a miracle? What molecules were being reconfigured in the man's eyes? What neurons were firing to effect this miraculous change? How did Jesus command cellular change at a microscopic level in order for the man to have his sight restored?

Jesus encountered the blind man and put mud on his eyes to begin a miraculous healing. The blind man could then see but everything was blurry. The man could have settled for this partial restoration however he must have known that it was not the perfect vision God was capable of delivering. So Jesus touched the man a second time and it was only then he could see perfectly. The man was entitled to a full healing if that was what he truly desired. And he did, he was not satisfied with a partial miracle.

The child who God is working to place in your home has likely received the first part of their miracle. They are in a safe orphanage, hospital, or foster home. They are still alive and receiving enough care to be sustained. But God has far more prepared for them. You are a part of that second touch in their lives. Through adoption they are moving from blind to impaired vision, and then from impaired vision to perfect vision. While they wait, not knowing if that second touch is coming, not knowing perhaps if it is even possible, you are part of God's miracle working power. All those obstacles you are facing, documents you are compiling, meetings you are attending – these are the details God is ordaining as part of your child's restoration into a loving family. Without your efforts, the fulfillment of adoption cannot occur and God's plan for this child will not be realized. Your child doesn't see all the work that is taking place behind the scenes. But he/she is surely dreaming of a full restoration!

*Journal*

There is a child depending on you for restoration into a family. God has ordained adoption, and will move mountains to allow for this child to be accepted into your family. But it will take dedication, work, and sacrifice on your behalf as well. What is your role in this process? How do you approach your responsibility in carrying out the steps necessary to complete God's work?

## Journal continued

## Prayer

*Father, thank you for calling me to adopt a child into this family. Give me the strength, wisdom, and excellence to carry out the steps You have called me to take in order to ensure this adoption is successful. Amen.*

Date:_____

## Exposed

## Hebrews 4:1-13

*Nothing in all creation is hidden from God's sight. Everything is uncovered and laid bare before the eyes of him to whom we must give account.*

Hebrews 4:13

The process of adoption exposes your family to many people who will examine the details of your lifestyle, assess your suitability to be a parent, and essentially judge your character and fitness as a mother or father. It can be an uncomfortable and vulnerable position to turn over so many details of your private life to people who are often strangers.

One of the more difficult confessions I made during our family's adoption was at the court hearing while in Africa. In the days leading up to our court appearance, so-called Christian radicals had been accused of stoning and burning alive people in the streets around the capital city. There was a mounting tension between various religious and political communities. Our attorney advised me that the judge who would hear the case was a devout Muslim and he would require me to make a declaration of my faith in court before deciding the fate of our adoption case. The growing fear in the pit of my stomach was that a public profession of a deep and intimate love of God through Jesus Christ as my Savior would negatively impact the adoption we had fought so hard to complete. I had to trust that God would honor my profession of faith before this Muslim judge. And so, on the evening of the hearing, I stood in a cramped, hot, humid, African court before a devout Muslim Judge and, standing next to the children God had called me to, I professed the depth of my love for God, the salvation of my soul through Jesus, and the calling of my Lord and Savior to love orphans in their distress.

God has called you to adopt. He did so, knowing everything there is to know about you. Everything. So when the people and agencies involved in the adoption process seem to pry into every tiny recess of your life, know that what they see God already knows. If there are genuine issues that would be concerning or cause your case to be difficult, it is much better for your family that these are brought to the light and worked through now, before you are responsible for the precious child God has intended you to love. While it may feel intrusive, good child placement agencies really do want to find adoptive parents for waiting children and are generally very good at working with, not against, prospective adoptive parents.

## Journal

What are the things that cause you to feel exposed when you think about God seeing them? What are some issues you want to intentionally offer to God for help, so that you will not be fearful when your life story is bare and exposed.

_____

_____

_____

_____

_____

_____

_____

_____

## Prayer

*Lord, help me to live my life in such a way that I have no fear of showing my genuine self to anyone who examines it. Amen.*

Date:_____

## AN UNLIKELY HERO

## JOSHUA 2:1-16

*But the woman had taken the two men and hidden them.*
Joshua 2:4a

You may encounter times when other people do not understand your decision to adopt and may even be unsupportive or question your ability to be an adoptive parent. People may be talking about your family's decision and perhaps in the least supportive and most critical manner. They may be filling you with fears and doubts regarding the difficulties and struggles associated with adoption. Perhaps sometimes you even question your own family's decision. Doubts might arise. Is our family too old, too young, too big or small, too…? The list of potential doubts can multiply exponentially in a very short time.

Rahab could be considered a most unlikely hero in the Bible. As a prostitute, many people probably had a number of not-so-nice things to say about her. She surely didn't fit man's expectations of being qualified to have a major role in God's plan for the two spies sent by Joshua. Despite what the world might have thought of her, God had a plan that included calling this unlikely hero to save lives. Regardless of what might have been rumored against her then, Rahab now holds an important piece of history in her life. (For some further exploration, check out Matthew 1:5 and see where Rahab fits into Jesus' family tree!)

The adoption process is filled with opportunities in which, whether with adoption agencies, the courts, or birth families, you might begin to feel that you have to convince the world that you are fit to raise a child and prepared to fill the role of a mother or father. Your life will be scrutinized by many eyes who want to know if you are qualified and capable of being an adoptive parent. A lot of people are talking about you and they are wanting to know if you are capable of carrying out the lifelong commitment to a child through adoption. Despite who or how many people question your desire to adopt, you have to continue to follow what God has called you to do.

One of the most startling occasions that someone questioned our family's ability to adopt occurred while we were in their birth country. We had been waiting several hours in long lines to obtain our daughters' foreign passports. A security officer approached and, without provocation or warning, began yelling about Americans adopting local children in an attempt to harvest their organs. I felt like a thousand scrutinizing, criticizing eyes were turned on me in that moment, despite our family having only the most loving intentions for our daughters. Our escort and driver calmed the security officer and deescalated the situation, but the unanticipated pressure of such harsh questioning and accusation by an uninvolved bystander left quite an impression.

I want to remind you that God has a few things to say about you too. Sometimes He is talking to you. He is also talking about you behind your back and just out of ear's reach. He is moving in the hearts and minds of those decision makers in your adoption. He is talking to a child in a most intimate way and telling them that their miracle is coming. It is coming in the form of *you and your family*. You are the human hero, supernaturally called, to bring this child into a loving, lifelong family.

## *Journal*

What concerns do you have about your readiness to adopt? Are there aspects of your life you need to change before welcoming a child into your family? What are your strengths that God is ready to use in this child's life?

_____

_____

_____

_____

_____

*Journal continued*

___

## Prayer

*God, help me to keep my focus on You. Keep my attention away from the distractions of doubt and fear. Let Your voice be the strongest voice I hear. Amen.*

*Date:*_____

## THE MOST EXCITING STORY

## 1 PETER 3:15-22

*Always be prepared to give an answer to everyone who asks you to give the reason for the hope that you have.*
1 Peter 3:15b

The story you are weaving as your family moves through each part of the adoption process is unfolding into a beautiful tale of love and sacrifice, hardship and hope, dedication and resilience. Your family's story will continue to develop and unfold well after the adoption is complete and your children are forever bonded into your lives. The story you will frequently reminisce and tell others, inspiring them, will be that of the events that brought you to a completed adoption. Telling and re-telling your family's story will never get old nor will it lose the robust excitement that has filled your heart since your initial steps on this journey.

Our family shares freely about our adoption journey. On one occasion I was in the Middle East and enjoying coffee and conversation with a new acquaintance. We chatted about everything from global politics to travel woes, from the weather to careers and family. At no time did faith or religion become an independent topic of conversation. However, when I shared about our family's adoption, this gentleman asked why we would go to such great lengths to adopt children. There was truthfully only one answer I could offer – I had known for years that God had called me to adopt and that it was His favor and guidance that lead our family to adoption. With a wide smile and tears in his eyes, this man explained to me that he was so happy to learn that he had found, in me, a Christian friend. His family had disowned him because of his faith in Christ and he had to move away from his home because he was caught attending a secret Christian church. We ordered more coffee and shared our love of Christ with each other, unhindered in our thankfulness for our own heavenly adoption, and encouraging one another as believers must.

Considering that the earthly adoption of a child in desperate need of a family is both a calling for Believers as well as a tangible model of our own adoption by a Heavenly Father into the kingdom of Heaven, how can we not be reminded of the most exciting story of adoption ever presented? Adoption is a story, an event, and an act of love that can cross all boundaries. Heavenly adoption can do all those things as well as bring each and every person into God's family.

So when we tell about our family's adoption experience with joy, excitement, anticipation, and fervor, it is important to recall that the greatest story of adoption ever presented is that of our heavenly adoption. That is the greatest story of all time and should be told freely, with both compassion and excitement, so that every person you and I encounter can learn about the same heavenly adoption which we have been gifted!

*Journal*

What opportunities do you have to share about your family's adoption where you can also share about your heavenly adoption? Are you prepared to share openly about both?

_____

_____

_____

_____

_____

_____

_____

_____

*Journal continued*

_____

_____

_____

_____

_____


*Prayer*

*Father, thank you for including me in the greatest story of adoption ever told! Provide me with opportunities to share about your love for each of us so that I can tell about your adoption offer of Salvation. Amen.*

# Waiting Homes

*A Plan for Heavenly Adoption*

First we must each come to the realization that every person is born with sin. The presence of sin is what makes us unsaved and separated from God. (Romans 3:23; Psalm 51:5; 1 John 1:8)

As a result of the sin in our lives, we face an eternal consequence – death. This is more than just physical death, but an eternal separation from God. (Romans 6:23; Psalm 51:4; Matthew 25:46; Revelation 20:15)

God provided a way for our sin to be pardoned. He came to earth as a human – Jesus – and was willingly killed as a sacrifice for our sins. Jesus' death paid for cost of our sins and provided each person an alternative to eternal death and separation from God. (John 10:15; 1 John 2:2)

Accepting the gift of salvation God provided for each of us through Jesus is a choice. Believing in Jesus as Lord, accepting in faith that Jesus has paid the penalty for your sin, and asking for His gift of salvation is all that is required to be adopted into God's Heavenly family. (Acts 16:31; Ephesians 2:8-9; John 3:16; John 14:6)

# Waiting Homes

## ABOUT THE AUTHOR

Michelle Cross-Frase enjoys life with her husband Vernon and their two daughters whom they have adopted from Uganda. At the writing of this book, their family is preparing to welcome a baby boy into their lives as well.

Formerly a lead crisis negotiator, police Sergeant, and college instructor, Michelle has transitioned her career to the field of Christian life coaching. Michelle has a post-graduate certification in pastoral counseling and has earned a Master of Arts in Counseling. She has continued to pursue professional counselor education, completing a psychological trauma specialty course in Israel.

Michelle has traveled to the Middle East, Africa, Central America and Europe, but her heart is at home with her husband and children, one lazy Beagle, a pair of yellow kitties, a small flock of blue-egg-laying chickens, and honey bees.

www.ingramcontent.com/pod-product-compliance
Lightning Source LLC
Chambersburg PA
CBHW061457040426
42450CB00008B/1395